£7.99

A Pillar Box Red Publication

Photography © Bigpictures.co.uk and Shutterstock.com

ISBN: 978-1-907823-11-4

Written by Martin Johnston

Designed by Duncan Drummond

we love you...

JLS

An Unauthorised 2012 Annual

CONTENTS

8: We Love You JLS Because…

10: What's on the JLS iPod?

12: What's in a name?

14: Spotlight on Aston

17: Spot the Difference

18: The Giant JLS Quiz

20: JLS' Best Mates

22: Spotlight on Oritse

24: Hair Today, Gone Tomorrow!

25: JLS Wordsearch

28: 10 Things You Didn't Know About JLS

30: Spotlight on JB

Staff Entrance

32: **The First Album**

36: **The Singles So Far**

38: **Flying Start - The Early Days**

40: **The A-Z of JLS**

42: **Spotlight on Marvin**

44: **Jack the Lad Style**

46: **The Second Album**

48: **Name That JLS Tune**

50: **Awards Galore!**

52: **Back in the Race**

54: **JLS by Numbers**

56: **Then and Now**

58: **Away From The Studio**

60: **Answers Page**

we ♥ love you... JLS

because...

... you're the best boy band in the world!

... your harmonies are incredible!

... of all the charities you support!

... your videos are the best!

... you always look amazing!

... you didn't need to win X Factor to be a huge success!

What's On T

Aston:
Usher
Beyoncé
Chris Brown
Michael Jackson
Boyz II Men

JB:
The Script
Michael Jackson
Beyoncé
Lionel Richie

e JLS iPod?

Marvin:
Beyoncé
Ne Yo
Craig David
Marvin Gaye
Michael Jackson

Oritsé:
Lauryn Hill
Lenny Kravitz
John Legend
Stevie Wonder
Prince

JLS – What's in a Name?

JLS just seems to suit the boys, but what does it stand for and how did it come about?

Originally the boys performed under the name of UFO (usually meaning 'Unidentified Flying Object' but chosen by the boys as 'Unique, Famous and Outrageous'), and that was the name they used when they first auditioned for The X Factor in 2008.

However, X Factor producers advised them to change the name as it was already being used by a well known heavy metal band.

So the boys decided on JLS, which stands for 'Jack the Lad Swing', combining the phrase 'Jack the Lad' and the style of urban music known as 'New Jack Swing'. Although 'Just Lads Singing' fits well too!

Spotlight on **Aston**

Full name:	Aston Merrygold
Born:	13ᵗʰ February 1988
Star sign:	Aquarius
Eye colour:	Brown
Family:	Five brothers and one sister
Fave films:	All the *Rush Hour* series, *Stomp the Yard*, *Bad Boys*, *Bad Boys 2*
First album bought:	Usher's *My Way*
Fave colour:	Blue
Fave food:	Tuna and pasta
Fave sport:	Football
Heroes:	Mum & Dad, Grandparents, Will Smith, Michael Jackson

Spot the Difference

Look at these two pictures of the lads - can you spot **10** differences?
Mark all the ones you find on the bottom picture.

Tip: use a good pencil so you can keep your annual in mint condition!

The **Giant JLS** Quiz

1. What was the original name of the band?

2. What is the name of JLS' second album?

3. What is the last song on that album?

4. What is Marvin's second name?

5. Which UK rapper features on the single *Eyes Wide Shut*?

6. And which single features US female rapper Dev?

7. What do the initials JB stand for?

8. Who did JLS lose out to in The X Factor final?

9. How many MOBOs did the band pick up at the 2010 show?

10. And how many BRIT awards did they win that year?

11. Which other X Factor contestant supported them on the 2010 summer tour?

12. What is Oritsé's second name?

13. And what is JB's second name?

14. What is the last song on the *JLS* album?

15. And what is the first song on that album?

16. Which band did Jay-Z famously say JLS would be as big as?

17. What was the name of the live DVD released in 2011?

18. What is Aston's second name?

19. *Love You More* was the official single in 2010 for which charity?

20. What girl's name is the title of the B side of the single *One Shot*?

Answers on page 61

JLS' Best Mates

As you would expect, JLS have already worked with some of the best artists in the pop business.

JLS also made a lot of friends when they appeared on *Everybody Hurts*, the Simon Cowell-produced charity single for the Helping Haiti project. Among the artists JLS rubbed shoulders with on that project were giants of the pop scene like Robbie Williams, Gary Barlow and Cheryl Cole, along with international megastars like Mariah Carey, Michael Bublé and Rod Stewart.

Their sixth single, *Eyes Wide Shut*, officially featured Tinie Tempah. The English rapper and Mobo award-winner already has two number one singles and a number one album, *Disc-Overy*, to his name.

DEEKAY, is a top Danish production team who worked on both the *JLS* and *Outta This World* albums with the lads. They've worked with pop artists worldwide and have helped create hits for Lil' Wayne, Sugababes, Diddy and Joe McElderry.

Spotlight
on **Oritsé**

Full name:	Oritsé Williams
Born:	27th November 1989
Star sign:	Sagittarius
Eye colour:	Hazel
Family:	Two brothers and one sister
Fave films:	*The Lion King, The Shawshank Redemption, Dream Girls, The Pursuit of Happyness*
First album bought:	Sisqo's *Unleash the Dragon*
Fave colour:	Red
Fave food:	Anything at Nando's
Fave sport:	Table tennis, especially against Marvin!
Heroes:	My mum, brothers and sister, Will Smith, Martin Luther King, Berry Gordy Jnr, President Obama

Hair **Today,**
Gone Tomorrow

The boys' haircuts have certainly changed a few times; here's a look at some of their styles:

Wordsearch

Can you find the words hidden in the grid?

L	D	P	M	G	L	L	I	G	Y	K	D	H
Q	R	E	C	O	R	D	S	N	B	M	L	N
R	W	X	Z	M	S	S	H	X	E	T	O	B
B	E	A	T	W	E	B	D	V	N	D	G	L
P	D	J	I	M	K	L	I	T	I	T	Y	U
B	B	N	U	S	R	J	D	L	V	N	R	E
J	G	H	R	O	M	L	C	D	R	D	R	S
D	A	N	W	H	T	A	N	X	A	K	E	V
Q	F	C	L	L	Y	D	I	O	M	P	M	A
P	Z	M	K	M	O	T	X	L	T	M	N	T
X	Q	H	C	C	L	V	H	X	L	S	N	T
J	W	T	L	I	V	E	E	M	H	I	A	U
E	S	T	I	R	O	M	V	K	M	H	W	O

ASTON	JACK	LOVE	RECORDS
BEAT	JB	MARVIN	RHYTHM
BLUES	JIVE	MERRYGOLD	SWING
GILL	LAD	ORITSE	WILLIAMS
HUMES	LIVE	OUTTA	

10 Things You Didn't Know About JLS

1. Oritsé was originally scouted by lots of other boy bands but, turned them all down because he wanted to create his own, original sound.

2. Aston has five other brothers...

3. ...but pity the poor girl, just one sister!

4. David Beckham is one of JB's favourite writers...

5. ...and so is President Obama.

6. Aston still has a crush on Mary Kate and Ashley, the Olsen twins!

7. Oritsé is a big fan of US comedy cartoon *Family Guy*.

8. Marvin rates washing cars on his own street as a kid as his worst ever job.

9. The first gig he ever attended was Michael Jackson's *Dangerous* tour in 1994.

10. All the boys love the chicken in Nando's restaurant!

Spotlight on JB

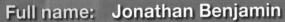

Full name: **Jonathan Benjamin Gill**

Born: **7th December 1986**

Star sign: **Sagittarius**

Eye colour: **Brown**

Family: **One brother**

Fave films: ***Training Day,
Gladiator,
Coming to America,
Bad Boys 2,
The Pursuit of
Happyness***

First album bought: **Backstreet Boys**
Backstreet's Back

Fave colour: **Yellow**

Fave food: **Chinese**

Fave sport: **Rugby to play,
football to watch**

Fave holiday: **Anywhere in the
Caribbean**

The **First** Album

Title: JLS

Release date: 9th November 2009

Length: 44:47

Record label: Epic

Producers: Wayne Hector, Steve Mac, J.R. Rotem, Fraser T. Smith, Jonas Jeberg, Cutfather, Metrophonic, DEEKAY, Soulshock & Karlin

Highest UK Chart position: Number one

Overseas: Number one in Republic of Ireland

Track list:

1. *Beat Again*
2. *Everybody In Love*
3. *Keep You*
4. *Crazy for You*
5. *Heal This Heartbreak*
6. *Close to You*
7. *Only Tonight*
8. *One Shot*
9. *Private*
10. *Don't Go*
11. *Only Making Love*
12. *Kickstart*
13. *Tightrope*

JLS – The Singles So Far

2009

Beat Again
The single which was the boys' first ever release went Gold in the UK and got to number one in the UK and number three in the Republic of Ireland.

Everybody in Love
The boys' second single from the JLS album also went to number one in the UK and in the UK R&B charts.

2010

One Shot
The third single from the JLS album, it reached number six in the UK charts.

The Club is Alive
The lead track from the album *Outta This World* became the band's third number one and their second single to also top the R&B charts.

Love You More
The second release from *Outta This World* gave JLS their second UK number one in a row.

2011

Eyes Wide Shut
The third single taken from *Outta This World* featured UK rap sensation Tinie Tempah and charted at number eight.

She Makes Me Wanna
Just released at the time of printing, this single featured US female singer and rapper, Dev.

Off to a Flying Start – UFO!
JLS – The Early Days

Around about 2006 people began to take notice of Oritsé's talents and he was approached by a number of boyband projects, but he decided he wanted to create his own band. He wanted a band whose members would have a real connection with each other, an idea taken from his heroes, Boyz II Men.

He met and recruited Marvin first, after being introduced through friends while he was in a band called VS. Aston joined next, and lastly JB, who was brought in for amazing harmonies.

The boys worked hard at bonding, found they had a lot in common and soon became good friends. They started out as a band under the name UFO which stood for Unique, Famous and Outrageous.

Working with production company New Track City they won their first award as the Best Unsigned Act at the Urban Music Awards in 2007.

In 2008 they auditioned for the fifth series of The X Factor and were advised to change their name... the rest, as they say, is history!

The **A-Z** of JLS

A is for...   Aston

B is for...   *Beat Again*, the first single

C is for...   Childline: Marvin is a patron of this charity

D is for...   DJ Triz, who produced their first ever release

E is for...   *Everybody in Love*

F is for...   Footie, the lads' favourite sport

G is for...   Grandparents, named by Aston as his heroes

H is for...   Hoodies, worn in different colours to identify the band

I is for...   In love, with JLS! – we all are!

J is for...   JB

K is for...   Kipling, as in Rudyard, one of JB's favourite authors

L is for...   Louis, (Walsh), mentor to the band

M is for...   Marvin

N is for...   National MS Society: Oritsé is a patron of this charity

O is for...   Oritsé

P is for...   Platinum, as in both albums!

Q is for...   Quality - a word which describes all of JLS' music!

R is for...   Rays of Sunshine: JB is an honorary patron of this charity

S is for...   Simon Cowell, Mr X Factor

T is for...   *The Club is Alive*

U is for...   UFO, the original name of the band

V is for...   Vivienne Westwood, Marvin's favourite designer

W is for...   Wii, the boys favourite games console

X is for...   X Factor, Series 8 - JLS were runners up in 2008

Y is for...   Yellow, JB's favourite colour

Z is for...   Jay-Z, a big fan of the band

Spotlight on **Marvin**

Full name:	**Marvin Humes**
Born:	**18th March 1985**
Star sign:	**Pisces**
Eye colour:	**Brown**
Family:	**Two bothers', Leon and Jackson**
Fave films:	*The Goonies, Back to the Future, The Matrix, Titanic*
First album bought:	**Michael Jackson's** *Bad*
Fave colour:	**Green**
Fave food:	**Nando's chicken**
Fave sport:	**Football**
Heroes:	**Mum & Dad, Michael Jackson, Martin Luther King**

JLS Style - Jack the Lads

The **Second** Album

Title: **Outta This World**

Release date: **19 November 2010**

Length: **48:07**

Record label: **Epic**

Producers: **Steve Mac, J-Remy, BobbyBass, Jerry Wonda, Toby Gad, Metrophonic, DEEKAY, Lucas Secon, Chris Braide, Fred Ball**

Highest UK Chart position: **Number two**

Track list:

1. *The Club is Alive*
2. *Eyes Wide Shut*
3. *Outta This World*
4. *That's My Girl*
5. *Work*
6. *I Know What She Like*
7. *Love You More*

8. *Other Side of the World*
9. *Better for You*
10. *Superhero*
11. *Love at War*
12. *Don't Talk About Love*
13. *That's Where I'm Coming From*
14. *The Last Song*

Name That **JLS** Tune

Can you identify these JLS songs with the words missing?

1. '... This Heartbreak'

2. 'Everybody in ...'

3. '... to You'

4. 'Eyes ... Shut'

5. 'That's My ...'

6. '... ... ... She Like'

7. 'Other Side of ... ...'

8. 'Don't Talk About ....'

9. '... For You'

Answers on page 61

Awards Galore!

In just four years in the music biz, JLS have racked up an amazing number of awards.

2007 (as UFO)
Urban Music Awards
Best Unsigned Act

2009
2 **MOBO** Awards inc
Best Song for *Beat Again*

**BRIT Awards nominated for
Best British Single**

2010
2 **BRIT** Awards inc
Best Single for 'Beat Again'

2 **MOBO** Awards inc
Best UK Act

2 **BT Digital Music**
Awards inc Best Group

2 **Urban Music** Awards
inc Best R&B Act

NME Awards nomination
for Best Band

"Back in the Race!"
JLS on The **X** Factor

Do you remember that famous night back in December 2008 when JLS didn't win The X Factor? All of us JLS fans were devastated at the time, but their talent has shone through and they've become just as big as they would have done if they had won the show! Let's take a look back at that series:

The boys auditioned for the fifth series of The X Factor in London and were an easy choice for the panel. As we've mentioned a few times in this annual, they had to change their name from UFO to JLS, though.

Louis Walsh was given the vocal groups that year and quickly took the boys under his wing, especially due to the fact that by the third week he had lost Bad Lashes and Girlband. In fact, JLS would constantly be referred to by all the judges as "the best band so far to be on The X factor."

In week seven they found themselves in the bottom two with Rachel Hylton, but were saved by Louis, Cheryl Cole and Simon Cowell. In week eight, their first performance was criticised by all the judges, but their second performance forced Simon to change his mind and he said, "You're back in the race." By week nine he was predicting a JLS win.

In the final, both JLS and Alexandra Burke performed the song *Hallelujah* and it was the female performer who won the public vote. However, as their joint clothing line shows, Alexandra and the boys have remained close friends.

JLS by Numbers...[1][2][3]

5...

...the series of The X Factor they entered in 2008

9...

...November 2009, release date of *JLS*, the first album

1...

...the number it reached on the UK, Irish and R&B Charts

317,000...

...the number of records it sold in 2010

75,000...

...amount in pounds JLS signed to Simon Cowell for

20...

...January 2009, the date that he changed his mind

One...

...*Shot*, the third single

1.2...

...million, the number of total sales of *JLS*, to date

30,000...

...in pounds, the amount the boys bid to record *She Makes Me Wanna* with producer Moe Faisal at Alicia Keys' Black Charity Ball in 2010

JLS Then and Now

Oritsé Williams in London.

Oritsé Williams decides to get into the music business to make money to help his mother who is suffering with multiple sclerosis. Recruits Marvin Humes.

Newly-formed UFO wins Best Unsigned Act at Urban Music Awards thanks to a mash-up of *Stand by Me* and *Beautiful Girl*.

27/11/86

30/08/94

2006

Early 2007

Late 2007

2008

Boyz II Men release *'II'* – an album which would have a huge influence on him and JLS.

Recruits JB Gill and Aston Merrygold.

UFO audition for The X Factor. They succeed but are asked to change their name. JLS (aka 'Jack the Lad Swing') is born. JLS come second, losing out to Alexandra Burke.

JLS almost sign to Syco, Simon Cowell's record label, but sign instead for Epic Records.

The first album, *JLS,* is released and goes straight into the charts at number one. The second single, *Everybody in Love* also goes to number one.

The second album, *Outta This World* released.

Jan 2009

Nov 2009

Nov 2010

July 2009

July 2010

May 2011

The first single *Beat Again* is released and goes to number one.

The Club is Alive becomes their third number one single.

She Makes me Wanna (feat. Dev) single released in UK & US.

Away From the Studio

When they're not rehearsing, writing or recording songs or on tour around the world, JLS are still really busy as a band. Here's a list of just some of the stuff they get up to:

TV... a documentary called *JLS Revealed* was shown on ITV2 on 7th November 2009, following nearly a year's worth of recording and touring since finishing The X Factor.

TV... an hour-long entertainment show, *This is JLS*, was shown on 11th December 2010, showing the boys performing their hits in front of a live TV audience.

Film... JLS were the first British music act to star in a 3D feature film. *JLS: Eyes Wide Open 3D* was filmed at the O2 Arena and was shown in over 3,000 UK cinemas in June 2011.

Fashion – The boys have created their own fashion brand with Alexandra Burke, called 2KX. The styles are as fresh and funky as you'd expect!

Charity - JLS spend as much time as they can working for charities across the UK and each of the lads does his own particular work:

Aston is a patron of Beatbullying.

Marvin is a patron of Childline.

JB is a patron of Rays of Sunshine children's charity.

And Oritsé was awarded with an Inspiration Award in April 2010 for his work with The Multiple Sclerosis Society.

SPOT THE DIFFERENCE (p.17)

Did you spot them all?

WORDSEARCH ANSWERS (p.25)

Did you search them all out?

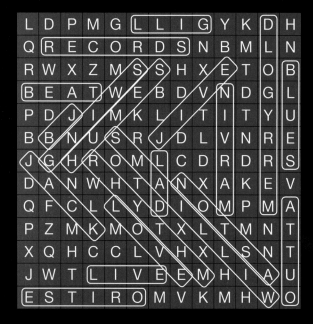

GIANT JLS QUIZ ANSWERS (p.18)

1. UFO
2. Outta This World
3. The Last Song
4. Humes
5. Tinie Tempah
6. She Makes Me Wanna
7. Jonathan Benjamin
8. Alexandra Burke
9. Two
10. Two
11. Diana Vickers
12. Williams
13. Gill
14. Tightrope
15. Beat Again
16. N'Sync
17. Only Tonight
18. Merrygold
19. Children in Need
20. Mary

NAME THAT JLS TUNE ANSWERS (p.48)

1. HEAL This Heartbreak
2. Everybody in LOVE
3. CLOSE to You
4. Eyes WIDE Shut
5. That's My GIRL
6. I KNOW WHAT She Like
7. Other Side of THE WORLD
8. Don't Talk About LOVE
9. CRAZY For You